SAVAGE AM ＿＿ＮＩ

# SAVAGE AMUSEMENT

Peter Flannery

REX COLLINGS
In association with the Royal Shakespeare Company
LONDON 1978

First published in Great Britain by
Rex Collings Ltd    69 Marylebone High Street
London W1

© Peter Flannery 1978

ISBN 0 860 36097 0

*Savage Amusement* was commissioned and first performed by the Faculty of Creative Arts, Crewe and Alsager College of Higher Education.

Typesetting by Malvern Typesetting Services
Printed in Great Britain by
Severn Side Printers Ltd.

*Savage Amusement* was first presented by the Royal Shakespeare Company at the Warehouse Theatre, London, on July 3 1978, with the following cast:

| | |
|---|---|
| OLLY | Charles Wegner |
| STEPHEN | Iain Mitchell |
| FITZ | David Threlfall |
| HAZEL | Jill Baker |
| ALI | Lesley Manville |

| | |
|---|---|
| DIRECTED BY | John Caird |
| DESIGNED BY | Chris Dyer |
| LIGHTING BY | Brian Wigney |
| SOUND BY | John Leonard |
| MUSIC BY | Mick Ford and Rob Hickson |
| STAGE MANAGER: | Susan Storr |
| D.S.M.: | Jane Tamlyn |
| A.S.M.: | Cathie Coulson |

# CHARACTERS

OLLY, 25
STEPHEN, 26
FITZ, 18
ALI, 20
HAZEL, 22

*"It is the minimum duty of a civilized society to protect everyone against harassment in his home, and arbitrary eviction."*
Richard Crossman, Minister of Housing, 1965.

# One

*(August. A downstairs room in a house in Rusholme, South Manchester. Two chairs, a low table, cushions, books, clothing. Enter STEPHEN slowly. He looks around the room. He examines some of the books on the floor. Enter FITZ. He is wearing a long overcoat and carrying a cardboard box full of tinned food. On seeing STEPHEN, he freezes. He puts the box on the floor, silently. STEPHEN stands and turns. They stare at each other.)*

STEPHEN This isn't what you think. There's only me. I'm looking for someone.

*(Without slackening his gaze, FITZ takes some provisions from inside his coat and puts them on the floor. He watches STEPHEN flatly and intently.)*

STEPHEN My name is —.

*(Fitz reaches into a deep pocket inside his coat and draws out a pick axe handle. He steps towards Stephen with the pick raised.)*

STEPHEN No.

*(Blackout.)*

# Two

*(A lecture theatre in darkness. Footsteps. A door is pushed open and swings closed.)*

OLLY Hello?

*(Light. He is revealed, holding a light cord. He looks round and begins to speak.)*

A long time ago, when they could see what was going to happen, our ancestors made prophecies. They said — and this is a quote —: Cities will progress and then decay to the ways of the lowest beings in them. Drinkers of dark liquids will come upon the land, speaking nonsense and filth.

[1]

Then the end will be near. Fathers will turn against their children, and children against each other. People will multiply until the cities can hold no more and will burst open. Then the streets will be filled with hate. And even when people are too weak to fight anymore, still the hate will continue. Then the stars will fall upon the land and boiling water rain upon the earth. Or the land will turn under and the sun won't rise to start the day. Then our possessions will turn into beasts before our eyes and devour us whole — and the end will have come at last. We will have brought it all upon ourselves and time alone will tell if any will survive.

*(The sound of footsteps, a man's voice, a dog. Olly turns out the light.)*

# Three

*(The house in Rusholme. Stephen is slumped in a chair, unconscious, with a sleeping bag rammed down over his head and shoulders. The contents of his bag and pockets are in a heap in front of him. Fitz sits opposite him, opening an unlabelled tin. Seeing that it contains tomatoes, he puts it down and selects another tin from the box at his feet. He shakes it and listens. He repeats this with another tin. All the while he keeps an eye on Stephen. Eventually he opens another tin, discovers that it contains beans, sniffs them suspiciously, and starts spooning them into his mouth. Stephen stirs. In a panic he starts to struggle. Fitz picks up his pick axe handle and gives the floor a whack. Stephen freezes for a while then slowly extricates himself.)*

STEPHEN  What happened exactly?

FITZ  You fainted.

STEPHEN  You didn't hit me?

FITZ  No. But I will.

STEPHEN  Oh. Don't let me interrupt your lunch. Or is it breakfast? I got in through a window.

FITZ  I know.

STEPHEN  You wouldn't like it if I stood up, would you?

*(FITZ raises the stick. STEPHEN stays where he is.)*

[2]

My name's Stephen Palmer. I suppose you know that by now.

FITZ    Never heard of you.

STEPHEN    I'm looking for my sister. The girl in the photo. I had an address in Whalley Range. When I got there it was empty but I found the owner who told me she'd gone to a squat and thought it was this street. I asked some people down the street who thought it was probably this house. I knocked. Her name's Alison.

FITZ    Don't know anybody called that.

STEPHEN    She's 20. Not very big. Brown hair.

FITZ    There's only me here.

STEPHEN    It's quite important. It's about her father.

FITZ    What about him?

STEPHEN    Do you know her?

FITZ    There's been different people here different times. I might be able to pass a message to her.
*(FITZ finishes the beans, puts the can on the floor and picks up the pick-axe handle. He is still seated.)*

STEPHEN    Why don't you just tell me where she is?

FITZ    Told you —I don't know.

STEPHEN    But you do know her?

FITZ    What's the matter with him?

STEPHEN    There's nothing the matter with him, he's just leaving and she's been out of touch for two years.

FITZ    *(Using the pick-axe handle to knock the tin out of shape.)* Leaving where?

STEPHEN    The country.

FITZ    What for?

STEPHEN    Look — if I gave you my phone number in London would you see it got to her?

FITZ    She might not be interested.

STEPHEN    I think if you know where she lives you should tell me. Then she can tell me herself if she's interested.
*(FITZ is still hitting the tin.)*

STEPHEN    Look, stop arsing about, will you? She lives here, doesn't she?

FITZ    I don't think you are her brother.

STEPHEN    So you do know her.

FITZ    I think this is your house.

STEPHEN    What?

FITZ    Come to try and get us out.

[3]

STEPHEN Look —

FITZ I think you've got a fucking nerve comin here. I think you should fix the roof instead of bustin in here.

STEPHEN I've told you who I am, now does Alison still live —?

*(FITZ demolishes the can and turns on STEPHEN.)*

FITZ Fucking liar! Bastards like you should be taught a lesson!

*(BLACKOUT.)*

# Four

*(A bridge over a road in Hulme, South Manchester. Heavy traffic. Hazel stands alone. She is trying to roll a cigarette but her hands aren't steady. After a while Ali joins her. Silence from them.)*

HAZEL It makes my stomach turn over. I'm sorry.

ALI Forget it. Let's go back.

HAZEL Forget it? Great.

*(Pause.)*

ALI I have to do some shopping.

*(Exit ALI. Fade.)*

# Five

*(The lecture theatre.)*

OLLY And time alone will tell if any will survive. Gloomy lot, weren't they? Not our ancestors of course. Good grief, no. Pueblo Indians. New Mexico. Filthy lot. In their personal habits, I mean. Savages. And as for their prophecies —! Well, I mean: stars falling on the land, boiling hot rain, streets erupting into hate and violence. It's all you get these days. Gloom, gloom, gloom. Why doesn't anybody look on the bright side anymore? Worse than the Sunday papers. Remember them? To hear some people talk you'd think the whole place was going to the dogs. Everybody knows everything's going to be all right as soon as we pull ourselves together and sort out these subversives. It's obvious. Unless you're a Pueblo Indian. Oh, sorry. Any Pueblo Indians here? Crikey, one, two, three . . . Guards, arrest those redskins! Take them back to their reservations. If they won't go there take them to my reservations. If that doesn't work —

VOICE *(Off.)* Oy!

OLLY Oh. Hello there.

VOICE What you doin in here?

OLLY Just talking. Bit of nonsense and filth.

VOICE Sounded like it.
*(The sound of a dog growling.)*

OLLY I like your dog.

VOICE Down, Rebel.

OLLY Is he a vegetarian?

VOICE Who said you could come in here? Are you a student?

OLLY Well it rather depends on whether the university is allowed to have me.

VOICE Right. Let's get movin.
*(The dog barks.)*

OLLY I only came to find out about next term.

VOICE Come on. Move.

OLLY Why is nobody around who can answer questions? Why isn't the library open? Look —

VOICE Up, boy!

OLLY All right.
*(He moves off. BLACKOUT.)*

# Six

*(The squat. FITZ is reading. A door slams, off. He covers the book. Enter ALI. He uncovers the book.)*

ALI Hi.

FITZ Hi.

ALI Hot.
*(FITZ nods.)*
Did I disturb you?

FITZ No. I was just havin a look at this.

ALI Ah. Make any sense?
*(FITZ looks doubtful.)*

[5]

Wouldn't mind a look at it later, if you like.

FITZ  Yeh.

ALI  Everything all right, Fitz?

FITZ  Yeh.

ALI  Do you want to be on your own?

FITZ  No.

ALI  Is Hazel in?

FITZ  Thought she went with you.

ALI  She did. We went to see some people in Hulme.

FITZ  Thought they'd stopped all that.

ALI  What?

FITZ  The centre.

ALI  They did. I just go round to a few people now and then to keep in touch. I thought I'd try and keep a bit of continuity. You never know — the centre might open up again.

FITZ  Yeh.

ALI  Except that it won't. Will it? You know Hulme better than I do.

*(FITZ shrugs.)*

A lot of the shops have closed down as well.

FITZ  They were closin when I lived there.

ALI  What a place, eh?

FITZ  Waste of time. You want to go and get yourself a proper job.

ALI  *(Amused.)* Proper job. Thanks a bunch, Fitz.

FITZ  You know what I mean.

ALI  I know exactly what you mean. What about you then?

FITZ  What?

ALI  What have you been doing this morning?

FITZ  Like what?

ALI  Like what have you been doing? It's not a trick question.

FITZ  Oh. I went to the shops.

ALI  In your overcoat?

FITZ  How d'ye know?

ALI  Bit conspicuous in this weather.

FITZ  Yeh.

ALI  Where is it then?

*(FITZ indicates his overcoat. She uncovers it.)*

ALI  Fucking hell, Fitz, you really gave Tesco a hammering this time.

FITZ  I got the tins off a bloke.

ALI  Erm. They haven't got any labels on them.

FITZ  You have to shake them. It's all supposed to be good stuff.

[6]

ALI    Could be anything. What was that one?

FITZ   Beans.

ALI    Don't you like beans or something?

FITZ   They're closin this weekend.

ALI    What — our Tesco?

FITZ   Bastards.

       *(Pause.)*

ALI    Do you take your stick with you?

FITZ   What stick?

ALI    Ever been caught?

FITZ   Loads of times. But they have to let you get to the door, see? So you just pile all the stuff onto the floor and piss off quick. All they want is the stuff back.

ALI    Can I have a biscuit?

FITZ   They're Hazel's. She asked me to get her some.

ALI    Ah. Better wait then. Has Olly not been back either?

FITZ   *(Shakes his head.)* I didn't know Hazel went to Hulme.

ALI    Well I'm hoping she won't make a habit of it. They've got enough problems. Unfair. How are you getting on with her — OK?

       *(FITZ shrugs.)*

       It was nice of you to let us come in here.

FITZ   I like Olly. He's good.

ALI    Where were you before this?

FITZ   Bout half a mile away.

ALI    Get kicked out?

FITZ   Got fed up. I get fed up — so if I see somewhere empty when I'm walkin about I have it.

ALI    Always on your own?

FITZ   Yeh.

       *(A door slam, off.)*

ALI    Hazel.

FITZ   Olly.

       *(Enter HAZEL.)*

FITZ   Shit.

HAZEL  Hello to you too, Fitz. Has Olly not been back?

FITZ   Not that I know of.

HAZEL  Wonder what that means.

FITZ   He's still out.

HAZEL  Yes, Fitz, I think we grasped that.

       *(She sees the biscuits.)*

       Ah, great. How much do I owe you?

       [7]

FITZ   Nothin.

HAZEL   No, come on. 35p.

FITZ   Didn't cost me anythin.

HAZEL   But —. Ah. Oh. Well, I expect they taste the same. Would you like one?

*(They both refuse.)*

I think Olly said he was going to the University to have a look for some books. He always comes back slightly weirder than usual when he goes there. He's trying to find out about bursaries as well. I'm absolutely knackered, Ali, I don't know where you get the energy.

ALI   Would you like some tea?

HAZEL   Love some. Fitz?

FITZ   Shall I do it?

ALI   It's all right.

HAZEL   Didn't manage to swipe any coffee I suppose?

FITZ   Didn't have any. Or tea either.

HAZEL   What's the world coming to?

FITZ   Oh, I forgot, Ali, there's no gas.

HAZEL   There's no what?

FITZ   Gas.

HAZEL   You mean no electricity?

FITZ   No. Gas. No gas.

HAZEL   Why not?

ALI   Have they disconnected us?

FITZ   Don't think so.

HAZEL   Are you sure? Did you check? Did you ask next door?

FITZ   No.

HAZEL   Why not?

FITZ   Cos I don't speak Swahili, do I?

HAZEL   Nor do they seeing as how they're West Indians.

FITZ   Whatever it is then.

HAZEL   English. They speak English, Fitz, like you and I.

FITZ   Yeh. But they smell.

HAZEL   You what?

FITZ   They're all dirty and they don't pay their rent.

HAZEL   Nor do we!

*(FITZ and ALI start laughing.)*

Oh, I see. Very funny. Were you joking about the gas as well?

*(They laugh even more.)*

[8]

Is there any gas or not?

FITZ  Seriously?

HAZEL  Yes.

FITZ  No.

*(Enter OLLY.)*

OLLY  That's what I like to hear.

FITZ  Hi, Olly.

OLLY  Fitz. Ah. Provender. Tesco?

*(FITZ nods.)*

ALI  And a bloke.

OLLY  Ah, one of Fitz's mysterious blokes. This boy will go far. Did you know it was closing, Ali?

ALI  Yeh.

HAZEL  I didn't know that. Christ. What for?

OLLY  Probably because Fitz has been nicking so much stuff. What's in here?

FITZ  Tomatoes. Didn't fancy them.

HAZEL  I just don't think it's funny anymore.

OLLY  What's that, Hazel?

HAZEL  The fact that there's practically nowhere to shop around here anymore. I just don't think it's funny. Why isn't anything being done about it?

OLLY  What would you like me to do?

HAZEL  It's just not a joke.

OLLY  You've said that three times. Let's take a raincheck on that. Fitz, Ali, do you think it's funny that all the shops are closing in our lovely garden suburb? No? Well that looks unanimous, Hazel.

FITZ  I'll put this lot in the kitchen.

*(Exit FITZ with the food.)*

OLLY  I feel like Fagin sometimes. Been out?

ALI  Hulme.

OLLY  You're my hero. Hazel too.

HAZEL  Have you been to the University?

OLLY  Yup.

HAZEL  Did you see anybody?

OLLY  Yeh, a bloke with a fucking big dog. I couldn't get any books. That's three weeks.

HAZEL  What's going on?

OLLY  Not sure.

HAZEL  You don't think they could be re-decorating the library or anything?

[9]

OLLY   No, I don't think that's very likely. It's a very weird feeling—there's hardly anybody about. Expect they're all in their summer cottages in Devon and Cornwall.

ALI   It was quiet in Hulme.

OLLY   Well that's more understandable. With all due respect, that place is obviously for the chop.

HAZEL   Oh fucking hell—why's everything depressing? It really pissed me off this morning, Ali.

ALI   Yeh, I know.
*(Enter FITZ.)*

FITZ   Gas is back on. I've put the kettle on.

OLLY   Hurray! And somehow the world seems a beautiful place.

ALI   A cup of tea makes all the difference.

OLLY   I should cocoa. Good news, bad news.

ALI   What?

OLLY   Bad news first.

HAZEL   If it's anything about power cuts or blackouts or frigging strikes keep it to yourself.

OLLY   Oh belt up, Hazel. Bad news. I've sold me car.

HAZEL   Oh, Olly!

OLLY   At least I've nearly sold it. There's no point hanging on to it. A guy in Longsight has promised me cash on Saturday.

FITZ   How much?

OLLY   £65.

HAZEL   Oh, no.

OLLY   It's all it's worth. Have you had a look at it lately? I can't afford petrol anyway.

ALI   What's the good news?

OLLY   Well, that leaves us with the car for one last day tomorrow, so good news: I've decided, or at least I put it to the democratic vote of this household, that we all pile into it one last time tomorrow and piss off to the seaside.

FITZ   Yeh!

OLLY   And we'll have a beano. Peeled tomato sandwiches, baked bean sandwiches, tinned surprise, the lot.

ALI   Great.

OLLY   And we won't talk about 'you know what' all day.

ALI   What?

OLLY   I'm sorry, I'm not at liberty to say. Is it a deal?

FITZ   Yeh.

OLLY   Well, Hazel, looks unanimous again.

HAZEL   I don't know what you're all looking at me for, I think it's a

[10]

bloody marvellous idea.
*(BLACKOUT.)*

# Seven

*(The squat, that night. OLLY and HAZEL. HAZEL slumped over a book, OLLY reading. Drumming from next door. Door slam. HAZEL stirs.)*

HAZEL   Olly?

OLLY   Thought you were asleep.

HAZEL   That'll be the day.

OLLY   Got to let them express themselves or else they'll stop paying their rates and start raping white women.

HAZEL   Was that the door?

OLLY   Fitz, I expect.

HAZEL   Going out or coming in? What time is it?

OLLY   *(Losing the thread of his book.)* Hazel . . .
*(Pause.)*

HAZEL   Let's go to bed, eh?

OLLY   You go. I want to finish this.
*(She leans over him and reads from the book under her breath.)*

OLLY   Hazel. Fuck off.

HAZEL   Guess what?
*(Silence.)*
I phoned Mum and Dad this morning.

OLLY   Hope you complained.

HAZEL   What about?

OLLY   Western civilization sliding into the abyss.

HAZEL   Forgot to mention it.

OLLY   I think your Dad should *do* something about it. I mean, he does work in a *bank*. Surely he could *do* something, instead of just sending us cheques. It's all very well but I've got my principles to consider. A kept man. The neighbours will rap.

HAZEL   Well I don't think you'll have to worry about that much longer.

OLLY   Oh. Tight-fisted swines. Perhaps we should have them to stay.

[11]

HAZEL   Oh yeh.

OLLY    Butter them up a bit. I could ask the guy next door to bone up on your mother's favourite drum solos if she let us know in advance. You and her could go shopping with Fitz, and your Dad and me'll go out and shoot a few elephants.

HAZEL   Are you remotely interested in what we talked about?

OLLY    Zip your lip.

        *(Enter FITZ.)*

FITZ    I got some coffee. I put the kettle on.

HAZEL   Oh, not just now, Fitz. That's smashing, honestly, but not just now thanks.

FITZ    Do you want some, Olly?

OLLY    Yes, please.

HAZEL   Olly . . .

OLLY    No thanks.

FITZ    I'll see if Ali wants some then.

HAZEL   Oh, for Christ's sake . . .

OLLY    *(To FITZ.)* We'll have one later, eh? With a biscuit.

FITZ    *(Exiting.)* Yeh. See you.

HAZEL   Why do you do things like that? You make me look a complete creep.

OLLY    Hazel, if you're going to get paranoid . . .

HAZEL   I'm not paranoid, I'm —.

        *(She stops dead.)*

        I don't want to argue about my mental state. I want to talk about my conversation with my Mum and Dad.

OLLY    *(Going back to his book.)* Fine.

HAZEL   They were talking about us maybe getting a proper house or flat.

OLLY    This is a proper house or flat.

HAZEL   You know what I mean.

OLLY    What?

HAZEL   Somewhere a bit more liveable in.

OLLY    Sounds revolting. They've stopped building country cottages in Rusholme.

HAZEL   *(Quietly.)* Talk to me about this, please.

OLLY    *(After a while.)* What are you saying? They're offering to buy us a house or something?

HAZEL   No, they're not. They haven't got that sort of money anyway. We didn't talk about it in detail. I dunno. I suppose they *might* help us with a deposit on a flat or something if we moved out somewhere and found jobs,

[12]

started living like normal human beings again.

OLLY  Is that what you'd like?

HAZEL  I don't know. What do *you* want?

OLLY  I'm asking you. Is that what you'd like?

HAZEL  Well we can't live in shanty town forever, can we?

OLLY  Why not?

HAZEL  Why not? Because we can't.

OLLY  Oh.

HAZEL  Olly, nobody lives here unless they have no choice.

OLLY  What is it you want that we haven't got?

HAZEL  Are you serious? Somewhere with a bit of privacy. That would do for a kick off.

OLLY  But we've never lived alone. There's always been somebody else. Ali for a bit, now Fitz as well.

HAZEL  We're married now.

OLLY  What difference does that make? I guarantee you that if we tried living alone I'd strangle you within ten minutes.

HAZEL  What sort of thing is that to say? What am I supposed to make of that?

OLLY  I'm reading my book.

HAZEL  Well, look. All right, maybe we have to live in this place for a while. But could we get out of this house?

OLLY  And go where? Another place the same. We haven't got any bread.

HAZEL  If we both get research grants we could easily afford to rent another place. You're just being stupid. Ali could come with us.

OLLY  What about Fitz?

HAZEL  He lives here. I'm not trailing Fitz round behind us for the rest of our lives, so forget it.

OLLY  If it wasn't for Fitz we could've ended up in a much worse place than this.

HAZEL  Well I'm sorry but I don't get on with him very well.

OLLY  Everybody guessed that, I think. Including Fitz. If he can put up with you, I'm bloody sure you can put up with him.

HAZEL  I'm not saying I can't put up with him, I'm saying I don't intend to share my life with him, thank you very much.

OLLY  What makes you think he wants you to?

HAZEL  You're so transparent, Olly. Just because a semi-literate eighteen-year-old looks up to you.

OLLY  We actually like each other. Difficult for you to understand, I know.

[13]

HAZEL   Bollocks. What is it about him that's so fantastic?

OLLY   We just have a lot in common.

HAZEL   I'm sorry, Olly, but you don't have anything in common. He's only a kid. Come on.

OLLY   He has a kind of strength we might be glad of. I like the way he looks at people, certain people. Well I don't like it, but I think I recognise it.

HAZEL   You pseud! I ask you a simple question and all I get is this arty-farty garbage. 'A kind of strength we might be glad of.' Wow.

OLLY   Piss off then. Ask Ali.

HAZEL   Why should I ask Ali? What does she know about him?

OLLY   Good question.

HAZEL   Fitz and Ali? You must be joking. You are joking, aren't you?

OLLY   Now how is it I can see that coming a mile off and you can't see it when it's pointed out to you?

HAZEL   Rubbish.

OLLY   You're stone blind, Hazel, because you're so fucking self-obsessed.

*(Pause.)*

HAZEL   Thank you. Anyway, this is all irrelevant. All I'm saying is this: why is it wrong for me to want to get out of this dump when you said yourself the whole place is for the chop?

*(The lights go out.)*

Shit! Well? Why is it wrong? I want to know. Olly.

*(There is a rustling.)*

Oh, fuck off! Get your hands off me, you cretin! Just forget I mentioned it. Piss off to bed. You make me fucking ill!

OLLY   *(Off, singing.)* 'It's only a shanty in old shanty town.'

Coming to bed or not, Hazel?

# Eight

*(A hill near the beach at Southport. Sounds of the sea, gulls. Enter ALI and HAZEL, out of breath. They look down to the sea.)*

HAZEL Olly was right. It's a good view.

ALI Beautiful.

HAZEL I don't know why we couldn't go on the sands like everybody else though.

ALI We can go down later.

HAZEL Fresh air. I'm not going back.

ALI Me neither. Oh, God, I'm hot though.

*(Enter OLLY and FITZ. They are carrying things for the picnic.)*

OLLY With only their machetes to aid them, Ollier and Kennedy hacked their way through the clinging, suffocating, primordial rain forest. The forest was the graveyard of explorers. It wanted to claim them for its own. But Ollier and Kennedy weren't the sort of guys to give up easily. They made one last despairing effort to hack their way out of the stifling verdant jungle. Ollier swung his mighty machete, the jungle fell away, and suddenly there it was before them: the aweinspiring thunder of the Pacific Ocean. I claim Southport for God.

ALI How about some of that lemonade?

OLLY Egad, Fitz. Natives. Don't move a muscle.

HAZEL Stop pissing about.

OLLY They're undoubtedly savage and probably extremely stupid. Let's make peace with them. I'll offer them lemonade and you shoot them in the back.

*(He takes out the lemonade and approaches them stiffly, holding it at arms length.)*

Take. Drink. Good.

*(ALI drinks.)*

The important thing is, old man, never let them see that you're afraid.

HAZEL Pass the carrier bag and we'll eat.

[15]

OLLY   Strange savage tongue. Do you think it could have been talking?

HAZEL   *(Going over.)* Oh, for fuck's sake.

OLLY   There it was again. It's probably some kind of crude language. I say, it's attacking our tuck.
*(He jumps on HAZEL and they roll around with HAZEL yelling abuse. FITZ joins ALI with the bags.)*

FITZ   Do you want something to eat?

ALI   Hurry up, you two, we want to eat.
*(Nothing but grunts and shrieks from them.)*
Have some of this.

FITZ   *(Taking lemonade.)* Ta. He's funny, isn't he? Why's he always on about natives? It's funny sometimes when you're in the street with him or in a shop. You don't half get some filthy looks when you're with Olly.

ALI   I know. He claims he studied anthropology. I think it's just because he's a loonie.

HAZEL   Why did you get your hair cut? You look like a bloody refugee?

FITZ   Has he ever been in a real jungle?

ALI   He's been to Brazil, I know, as part of a crew making a film. I suppose that was the jungle. You'll have to ask him. I think it was an American thing. He's not an intrepid explorer, I know that.

OLLY   Don't pull my hair. Don't pull my hair. You vicious — !

HAZEL   Say you're sorry then. Say you're sorry!

FITZ   Brazil. I drew a map of it once at school.

OLLY   Now look Hazel, I'm serious, I'm warning you.

HAZEL   Now look, Hazel, I'm serious . . .

FITZ   Brazil. Hey, Olly. What's it like in Brazil?
*(More fighting, abuse, rolling around.)*

ALI   Let's have a sandwich. We're starting.
*(They take a sandwich.)*

FITZ   Did you hear them shouting last night?

ALI   Who didn't?

FITZ   I don't think Hazel likes it. She hates me.

ALI   Oh rubbish. Hazel couldn't hate anybody.

FITZ   If her and Olly went would you go as well?

ALI   I don't know. I wouldn't go just because they went. They might not want me to.
*(OLLY and HAZEL have stopped fighting and are necking instead.)*

[16]

FITZ  Hey, Olly?

OLLY  What?

FITZ  What's it like in Brazil?

OLLY  What's what like in Brazil?

FITZ  Things.

OLLY  Sex was fantastic.

HAZEL  You—!

*(She starts to hit him again.)*

OLLY  Purely from the point of view of scientific observation.

HAZEL  Pervert.

FITZ  What's it like in the jungle?

OLLY  Bit awkward. No room to lie down.

FITZ  No, come on, what's it like?

OLLY  Why this sudden upsurge of interest in Brazil?

FITZ  Ali says you made a film.

HAZEL  Oh, here we go—Antonioni. He was only carrying the cook's pots and pans.

OLLY  I'm warning you, bag features!

*(He makes a sudden move and she catches him with her knee squarely in the groin by accident. He doubles up.)*

HAZEL  Oh, I'm sorry, Olly.

*(Fade.)*

# Nine

*(Later that afternoon. They have finished the picnic and are lazing. HAZEL lies with her head in OLLY's lap.)*

OLLY  I still think about it quite a lot. It's a beautiful place. Magnificent. And the people. I made quite a few friends.

FITZ  Americans?

OLLY  No, they were basically a bunch of turds. The indiginous natives. Various ones I met.

ALI  Sounds like a great place.

HAZEL  You still dream about some of them, don't you, Oll?

OLLY  Yeh.

HAZEL  I'm sorry. Wasn't I supposed to say that? Can't do much right today. Are you all right?

OLLY  Just keep your head still.

ALI    What do you dream about?

OLLY    One or two of the people I got to know well. It's their way
of keeping in touch.
*(There is a long silence.)*

FITZ    Eh?
*(Laughter.)*

HAZEL    Better than the phone anyday. Let's go for a swim!

ALI    *(Jumping up.)* Yeh!

FITZ    Yeh! I can't swim.

HAZEL    We'll teach you. Come on, Kenneth.
*(They are on their feet, except OLLY.)*

OLLY    Nah, not for me.

HAZEL    Oh come on.

OLLY    No.

HAZEL    Why not?
*(ALI and FITZ are half way out.)*

OLLY    I don't want to.

HAZEL    Why not?

OLLY    I don't want to.

FITZ    Oh well, I'll stay as well then.

ALI    Let's all stay. We'll sunbathe.

HAZEL    Oh, terrific.

OLLY    *(Jumping up.)* OK. Looks like me and you, then Hazel.
*(He bustles her out. ALI and FITZ look at each other, a bit
embarrassed.)*

ALI    Mad as a hatter.

FITZ    What would you like to do?
*(Fade.)*

# Ten

*(Later that evening. ALI is resting her head on FITZ's lap.
Enter OLLY and HAZEL in silence. ALI and FITZ separate.)*

ALI    Hi.
*(HAZEL starts to pack things away, though not hurriedly.
You don't look very wet.*

OLLY    No, we just paddled. Water was cold. Thought the Pacific
was supposed to be warm. Nice time?

ALI    Just talking. Watching the sun.

[18]

*(OLLY gives them a stage wink.)*
Getting a bit nippy, isn't it?

HAZEL  We can go back whenever anybody's ready. I don't mind.
I'm quite happy to sit.
*(Which she does, facing the sun and the sea.)*

ALI  Oh. We've lost some tiles at the back. So Fitz says he
might start sleeping downstairs when the weather turns.

OLLY  Good idea. Would you like us to move downstairs and you
have our room?

FITZ  Nah.

HAZEL  We will if you want.
*(FITZ shakes his head).*

ALI  I feel so sleepy. I've had a great day. Thanks, Olly.

FITZ  Yeh, I've had a great day. It was a great idea.

ALI  I hope the lights will be on when we get back. And the
water.

OLLY  Water?

ALI  Water was off in Hulme this morning. Been off since
yesterday afternoon. No warning or anything.

OLLY  Why?

ALI  No reason. Nobody gives a shit. Goes on all the time.

FITZ  Erm . . . would it be all right if you could drop me in Hulme
on the way back? I've got to see a bloke.

OLLY  Taking those tomatoes back?

ALI  It'll be dark.

FITZ  Yeh. You better not wait for me. You'll get a brick through
the windscreen.

ALI  I mean you.

FITZ  Nah, I'll be all right.

HAZEL  You're braver than me. That place is a running sore. You
wouldn't get me going there on my own even in daylight.

ALI  Some people have to.

HAZEL  Since when?

ALI  I'm talking about the people who live there.

HAZEL  Beg your pardon.

OLLY  Might as well face it—if anything was going to be done
about that place it would've happened by now.

FITZ  I know what I'd do. I'd blow Hulme to bits then dig a
bloody great big hole in Moss Side and shovel it all in.

OLLY  Then what?

FITZ  Nothin.

[19]

OLLY   Not very constructive, but positive. Wouldn't surprise me a bit if that's exactly what they had in mind.

HAZEL   I agree with him. Pull it all down and start again.
*(To ALI.)*
You find that funny, do you?

ALI   No, I don't.

HAZEL   You might as well know, Ali, I'm not going back to that shit heap.

ALI   Fine. I never asked you to come in the first place.

HAZEL   Beg your pardon again. I thought you wanted me to help out.

ALI   We got a crossed line somewhere then.

HAZEL   Fine. As long as we know where we stand.

OLLY   What's going on here?

ALI   Oh. It's this family we saw in Hulme yesterday. They're all in a bad way, particularly the wife. The bloke drinks. The flat's erm . . . indescribable. Basically he took exception to one of Hazel's comments and was abusive to her. Not surprisingly when you think about it. That's all.

HAZEL   That is not all, Ali. That kid's face was a mass of bruises. He must've been using him as a punchbag.

ALI   Well what do you expect me to do about it?

HAZEL   You could at least have told him what you thought of him. He's a fucking psychopath.

ALI   It doesn't matter what I think of him. What does matter is that you got him so worked up he probably spent the rest of the day punching somebody else. Most likely his wife.

HAZEL   That's a vicious thing to say.

ALI   Course it's vicious. The place they're living in's vicious.

HAZEL   Does everybody in the place have to behave like an animal?

ALI   That's typical of the kind of mindless remark . . .

HAZEL   I didn't mean Fitz. I was not talking about Fitz. I was talking about people living there *now* and anyway —

OLLY   Shut your face, Hazel.

HAZEL   Look, Olly, I wasn't talking about —

OLLY   All right. All right.
*(Silence.)*
I had no joy at the University again today. It's beginning to look like bad news for the good guys.

ALI   You don't think they won't open it up?

OLLY No, I can't see them not opening the University. There'd be a riot. When there's unrest the best thing to do with students is let them study. But those cuts obviously aren't going to be restored. There was a big fuss at first. Cutting back on social sciences, humanities, arts, etcetera, but nothing's going to be done about it. It's happened. It's going to get worse more likely than not. All the faculties' big promises about funding students directly have just evaporated. They haven't got the money. It was talk. They'll be hard pressed to keep their regular courses intact. There'll be nothing left over for silly buggers like me to research into a load of wop Indians. Or seventeenth century Spanish literature.

HAZEL Is that what you think?

OLLY Yeh. That's what I think. Shall we go?
*(Fade.)*

# Eleven

*(October.*
*An office of the DHSS. A compartment with a chair in it.*
*The other side is obscured by a very fine grille, almost*
*opaque. The voice of the clerical assistant is amplified.)*

VOICE Mr and Mrs Ollier section four please.
*(Enter OLLY and HAZEL. HAZEL sits, OLLY stands. They*
*look into the grille without much success.)*

OLLY I've heard of Social Security but this is ridiculous.

VOICE Can I help you?

OLLY We'd like to claim supplementary benefit.

VOICE I see. Can I have your address please?

OLLY Yeh. 18 Agnes Street, Rusholme.

VOICE How long have you lived there?

OLLY Three months.

VOICE Are you the householders?

OLLY No.

VOICE Are you the legal tenants?

OLLY Depends what you mean by legal. Don't I know you from somewhere?

VOICE  Do you have a rent book?

OLLY  No. The voice is very familiar, you know.

VOICE  Do you live there with the active consent of the owners?

OLLY  Nobody's tried to throw us out.

VOICE  Do you live there with the active consent of the owners?

OLLY  Oh, I see what you're driving at. No.

VOICE  What do you do for a living, Mr Ollier?

OLLY  I'm in movies.

VOICE  Are you working at the present time?

OLLY  No.

VOICE  Does your wife work?

OLLIE  Why don't you ask her—she's only sitting here?

VOICE  Do you have an occupation, Mrs Ollier?

HAZEL  Not really. I was hoping to do research at the University.

VOICE  I see.

HAZEL  We both were.

OLLY  But the government has decided to cut money for education and build tactical nuclear weapons for use in inner cities.

VOICE  I see. Are you both registered with the Employment Exchange?

OLLY  Yes, thanks. We just spent a lovely morning there. Were you at a party my place last Saturday?

VOICE  Did the Employment Exchange register you as unemployed persons?

OLLY  Well, no, there was some dispute about this. Apparently unemployed doesn't mean unemployed anymore.

HAZEL  Olly—.

VOICE  Have either of you held a job in the UK of more than three months duration within the last three years?

OLLY  Well, no, this is the problem, you see—

VOICE  I'm afraid you don't qualify for benefit while you're not registered as unemployed if you're occupying unauthorized accommodation.

OLLY  Don't houses count?

HAZEL  We're looking for another place.

VOICE  If you'd like us to send you a leaflet explaining your rights and responsibilities in this matter we'd be pleased to.

OLLY  This leaves us in a bit of a ticklish situation, you see. We're skint.

VOICE  Alternatively, I'd be happy to answer any questions you may have concerning the general workings of the benefit scheme. Is there anything you'd like to ask?

OLLY  Yeh. Do you have a mole on your left thigh?

*(Silence.)*

Hello?

HAZEL  You stupid fart.

*(Blackout.)*

# Twelve

*(The squat. ALI and FITZ with a book.)*

ALI  What's that then? What is it?

FITZ  I dunno.

ALI  Yes you do. We've done this. Go on. Go on. I haven't got all day.

FITZ  Gooz. Goose?

ALI  No. You don't say the 'u' when it comes before an 'e' like that remember?

FITZ  Oh, yeh, yeh. Guess.

ALI  Right. What does the sentence say then? What's he saying?

FITZ  We can guess what is in the pa-ket. Packet.

ALI  Good. Not bad, eh?

FITZ  They seem to do the same things over and over, don't they? It's hens and balls, cats and dogs, mummies and daddies.

*(Door slam, off. ALI and FITZ put space between them. Enter HAZEL and OLLY. OLLY is reading a handbill and carrying a letter.)*

ALI  How did it go?

HAZEL  Zero. I thought at one point we were going to get the firing squad never mind supplementary benefit.

ALI  Not much point in me going then.

HAZEL  No. You have to have a job to count as unemployed apparently.

FITZ  I dunno why you bothered.

OLLY  Listen to this crap.

HAZEL  What is it?

OLLY  It was on the mat. Or on the floor where the mat used to be

[23]

before Fitz put it between two slices of bread and had it for his breakfast. Oh, sorry, Ali, this is for you.

*(He tosses her the letter. From next door, the sound of drums.)*

HAZEL   Don't his arms ever get tired?

OLLY   Listen to this for Arsehole-Of-The-Year Award. From the North West Area Public Services Committee. Who? We beg to remind all occupants that it is a criminal offence punishable by fines and imprisonment for any un-authorized person to reconnect or attempt to reconnect or otherwise tamper with in any way any supply of gas, electricity or water which has been lawfully disconnected by the relevant authority. Blah, Blah. It is an offence — get this — it is an offence to enter and occupy vacant property in those areas designated by the North West Area Public Execution Committee as clearance areas. These areas are shaded blue. Where? That's a fat lot of help. Where are people supposed to live — disused mine shafts? I wonder if this lot's gone out in Hulme. I bet it has you know. It's not just neglect now, they've made their minds up. What's the matter, Ali? Bad news?

*(ALI looks angrily at FITZ.)*

ALI   That was a nice thing to do. It's from my brother. Posted ages ago.

HAZEL   Is everything all right, Ali?

ALI   I'm just going to try and find a phone that hasn't been smashed to bits.

*(Exit ALI. Fade.)*


# Thirteen

*(The park. OLLY and ALI sitting.)*

OLLY   Is that him?

ALI   No.

OLLY   That him?

ALI   He's 26, not 86.

OLLY   Exciting, isn't it? I don't think I've ever actually met a bureaucrat. Fancy keeping him a secret.

ALI   I want you to push off when he arrives.

[24]

OLLY  What? But I want to see it all. Two years. Long time, you know. Expect he's quite different. Sure that wasn't him?

ALI  Cut it out, will you?

OLLY  Sorry. I'll go.

ALI  Go and do something useful.

OLLY  Like what?

ALI  Help Fitz with the shopping.

OLLY  Nah, I'd be hopeless. I mean, I'd blush. We'd get caught.

ALI  I'm serious.

OLLY  So am I.

ALI  He's nicking much more stuff than he used to.

OLLY  Look, I don't ask him to. It makes him feel good. Come on, Ali, give me a break.

ALI  No, I won't give you a break. He's doing it because of us and it's stupid. We should tell him there's no need.

OLLY  But there *is* need.

ALI  We'll survive.

OLLY  All right. What am I supposed to say? ''Look here, son. Ali, Hazel  and I want you to stop all this shoplifting nonsense.''

ALI  Oh forget it. I'll say something to him myself.

OLLY  Come on, Ali, I don't want to fall out with you.

ALI  I don't want to fall out with you. We're not going to fall out.

OLLY  Good.

ALI  But I mean it.

OLLY  What exactly?

ALI  We must be careful—all of us—not to take advantage of him.

OLLY  This is grotesque. You're talking about me, I take it.

ALI  All of us.
*(Pause.)*

OLLY  Let me tell you something. You know, and I know, that Fitz will still be here long after we've left this place.

ALI  *I* don't know that.

OLLY  That he belongs here and we *don't. He* knows that too.

ALI  No, he *doesn't*, Olly. He doesn't understand it.

OLLY  So if and when he decides he'd be better off on his own, he'll go. No messing. He'll just go.

ALI  You think so?

OLLY  Of course he will. And good luck to him. He can't carry passengers.
*(Pause.)*

[25]

ALI    I almost wish you were right. But you're wrong.

OLLY    Fair enough. Now. The question they're all asking back at the house is: is your brother Stephen as big a prick as he sounds?

ALI    There he is.

OLLY    Which one?

ALI    With the rucksack.

*(OLLY looks, nods slowly, exits extravagantly. Enter STEPHEN.)*

STEPHEN    Hello.

ALI    Hello.

*(Stephen looks around suspiciously.)*

ALI    What are you looking for?

STEPHEN    Is it safe to assume that nobody's going to jump me? I mean, if I sat on the bench, it wouldn't blow up or anything?

ALI    Can't guarantee it.

STEPHEN    Only the last time I came to see you I got attacked.

ALI    So I heard. That's what happens when you break into someone's home.

STEPHEN    He's a friend of yours then?

ALI    Yes.

*(Pause.)*

How are you?

STEPHEN    How am I? Fine, thanks. You?

ALI    Fine.

STEPHEN    You don't look it.

*(Pause.)*

I talked to the old man yesterday after you 'called. He was over the moon. Sends you his love.

ALI    That's nice. Maybe I'll write to him.

STEPHEN    He'd appreciate that, I think.

*(Pause.)*

Did I just pick a bad day or . . .?

ALI    Any day would've been a bad day. I don't know if I can handle all this.

*(Pause.)*

STEPHEN    I've been wanting to come to Manchester for a long time. Capital of the North and all that. I had a little look round in August. I'd like to see some more. Maybe you could take me to Hulme.

[26]

ALI   I didn't ask you to come barging back into my life like this.

STEPHEN   No. But I'm here now so why not make the best of me? Will it be all right if I stay a few days?

*(ALI nods, almost laughing.)*

ALI   Stay as long as you want.

STEPHEN   When you get sick of me, just tell me to fuck off. I'm used to it.

ALI   You look a bit older.

STEPHEN   Occupational hazard.

ALI   What's it been like?

STEPHEN   Bad.

*(Fade.)*


# Fourteen

*(A bright light shines into FITZ's face. He is sitting in a chair. Nothing else is visible. An amplified voice speaks to him.)*

VOICE   All right, piggy, let's hear you.

*(FITZ looks around but can't see anything because of the intense light.)*

VOICE   No use looking for me, you silly bastard, I'm somewhere else. I'd come in there with you only I couldn't stand the stench. Now what have you got to say for yourself?

FITZ   What do you want me to say?

VOICE   Make a habit of it?

FITZ   What?

VOICE   Shoplifting. Do you make a habit of it?

FITZ   I was just walkin along the road and this van pulls up —

VOICE   You don't have to tell me, I was driving the bloody thing. The management of Tesco supermarket, Longsight, observed you helping yourself to their property, challenged you, whereupon you threw a pocketful of tinned food down onto the floor and left the premises. It was your hardlines we were patrolling when the call came in. I wish you could've seen your face, son. You see the time has now passed when light-fingered lennies like you can just hand the stuff back and clear off.

[27]

FITZ  I was goin to buy it.

VOICE  Oh, please, don't insult my intelligence, son, I'm not a lady magistrate. What's your name?

FITZ  Fitz.

VOICE  Fritz what?

FITZ  Fitz. Short for Fitzgerald.

VOICE  Fitzgerald what?

FITZ  Sir.

VOICE  Right. Go on. You never know—we might grow to like you.

FITZ  Me full name is John Fitzgerald Kennedy. I'm called after an American president who got killed just when I was born. Somebody shot him. Do you want me to . . .?

VOICE  Some of my friends think you're making this up. You wouldn't do that, would you?

FITZ  No, sir.

VOICE  All right. Keep going till I ask you to stop.

FITZ  I saw it on a film on the TV. He was in his car with all his guards. They were visitin Russia. His wife was with him. He got shot in the head by a Communist. I don't really know why I'm called after him.

VOICE  We don't want a history lesson. We want to hear about you. What do you do?

FITZ  I dunno what you mean.

VOICE  Are you thick? All right. Where were you born? Do you know that?

FITZ  We lived in Moss Side. When I was born. There was me, me Mum and Dad, me brothers Sean and David and me sister Elizabeth. Me brothers were both older than me and me sister was younger. Moss Side wasn't anything like it is now. This was before they changed it. It was startin to go downhill but we lived in a pretty good house near The Prince of Wales—

VOICE  You'd have thought he'd be a bit more choosey.

FITZ  *(Careful as ever not to interrupt.)*—near the Anvil Brewery. It used to stink the house out when the wind blew in the wrong direction. The house was really old. We had mice and one of the bedrooms was damp but it seemed all right to me apart from that.

VOICE  Very interesting. Carry on.

FITZ  We lived there till I was nine. Me Dad worked for Kraft Margarine. Trafford Park. Me Mum used to work part-time

[28]

cleanin in Princess Road School. Then when I was about
nine —

VOICE Just a minute.
*(Fade.)*


# Fifteen


*(In the park. STEPHEN and ALI.)*

STEPHEN We've got a pretty clear idea now what's going to happen
to the people at the bottom. Christ, what happened to
them under so-called socialist governments was bad
enough. And if I didn't know it before, I certainly know it
now after nine months in Housing. I thought my job was
to help solve the housing problem in London.

ALI Wasn't it?

STEPHEN No. I had to watch so-called public servants searching for
technical reasons to leave homeless families on the streets.
I didn't just have to watch it, I had to be part of it. Denying
accommodation to families entitled to it by law — though
they won't have to worry about that for long thanks to
their new masters. Shunting families around from one area
to another to try and evade their responsibilities. Blatant.
Sending people to uninspected temporary accommodation. Using guest houses, caravan sites, old
workhouses, police stations, old dormitories — all totally
inadequate accommodation — as dumping grounds for so-
called problem families until I began to wonder if it wasn't
them that was the problem but us. Me. Having dumped
these people I was required to impose punitive restrictions
which were specifically designed to make any semblance
of normal family life impossible for them. I mean it wasn't
just immoral, it was bizarre. We've had large-scale
squatting in London now for twelve years. It's become part
of the housing picture. We were now supposed to revert to
the initial authoritarian response — which never worked first
time round — of sending in teams of thugs to wreck
property and render it uninhabitable. It was a bad dream.
My job was to destroy houses. Anyway, I didn't have long
[29]

to ponder my dilemma because they sacked me. It's nearly twenty years since Rachmann, the new Rent Act, security of tenure, Rent Tribunals, all that. For twenty years people have been deluding themselves that somehow progress was being made quietly. By this time last year I would reckon after all the talk it had got roughly twice as bad. And it's taken all this time but it looks like we've finally got a government which has decided to tackle not just housing but all the problems of the inner cities. It's going to screw them into the ground.

ALI   So now you're out of a job and preaching to the converted.

STEPHEN   I've been driving an ice cream van this summer.

ALI   It's a disgrace.

STEPHEN   Come off it. An elitist like me? Things will start moving again soon anyway. It's time to start organizing effective opposition. There are going to be some new rules invented this time.

Al   Same game though.

STEPHEN   It's not a game.

ALI   But you enjoy it all.

STEPHEN   Not enjoy.

ALI   The opposition, I mean. The organization. Fighting. I envy you it. Do you know—you're exactly the same. I mean, *exactly* the same.

STEPHEN   Good.

ALI   Weird.

STEPHEN   Why? Because I don't eat cold beans out of tins? Or do funny walks in the park like your friend over there?

ALI   What? *(She spots him.)* Olly! Go home! Go home! *(He goes.)* No. Because everything else has changed and you haven't. Nothing to be proud of. Just means you're probably still a schmuck.

STEPHEN   I don't have to sit here and be insulted.

ALI   You could come home and be insulted.

STEPHEN   In for it, am I?

ALI   Expect so. Still, you're tough. You can take it.

STEPHEN   That's right. You've changed quite a bit.

ALI   Of course I have. I was a baby when I left home.

STEPHEN   The old man's changed. Two years is a lot of time at his age. You'll see a difference.

ALI   Will I?

[30]

STEPHEN  Yes. If you come.

ALI  If I do, it'll be as much to see Catherine as Dad.

STEPHEN  I didn't think you were specially fond of her.

ALI  I wasn't specially fond of her.

STEPHEN  She seems a bit happier than she used to. Maybe it's just I don't see so much of her.

ALI  When did they go to Scotland?

STEPHEN  Eighteen months ago. He retired early because he didn't like the look of things.

ALI  That doesn't sound like him at all. Makes you feel creepy.

STEPHEN  He just got old.

ALI  Then why's he decided now to go to Canada? Why not get another job here? He's copped out, hasn't he?

STEPHEN  Well, I think he copped out years ago, but . . .

ALI  Dad's aren't supposed to do that.

*(Fade.)*

# Sixteen

*(Intense light on FITZ.)*

VOICE  All right. Sorry, Fritz, I needed a run off. Carry on. You're nine years old and everything's about to go for a burton, I expect. Come on. Don't be shy.

FITZ  Erm. Me Dad lost his job in Kraft's and he couldn't find another one. About the same time the corporation demolished the house and gave us a new flat in Hulme.

VOICE  But not necessarily in that order.

FITZ  No. Other way round. It wasn't very far away and me Mum was happy about it cos she said it was cleaner and anyway the Moss was goin downhill cos of all the students livin in it and prostitutes and that. Erm. I didn't much like the new flat. It was pokey. And it was too high up. There was nowhere proper for the kids to play and the three of us brothers had to share a bedrom. I can't remember why. Oh yeh, there was all this green mould. Me Dad couldn't find a job and things never seemed to get back to normal. Me Mum packed up her job cos it turned out we was better off if she didn't work. Things just kept gettin worse though. Money was a problem in the old house. I remember them

[31]

arguing. Then they got into debt when we moved into the flat because they wanted new furniture and things. The old stuff looked tatty in the new flat so we chucked it nearly all out. I don't think they knew the flat was going to cost so much. Nobody did. When the bills for heating started comin in I remember it caused a big fuss not just in our house. They just didn't have enough money. I think they knew things weren't going to get any better. As far as I remember after we moved into Hulme me Dad never worked again. Everything just ground to a halt. The debts piled up and they started to cut off the power and everythin because we couldn't pay to have it. We tried to stick together but it was useless. There was a lot of pressure on me Mum and Dad. Everybody seemed a bit barmy. Sean and David went to live with me auntie in Scotland. We all pretended it was just a holiday until things got better. But we knew it wouldn't. Me Dad started boozin and that was the end of that. The flat was in a shockin state. I used to stay out. Kip outside. We had no water or anything. Once they interviewed me Mum for the paper and they said this is a woman at the end of her tether. There was a picture of me. In 1978 me Mum had a nervous breakdown and went into hospital at Withington. Me dad disappeared and I've never heard of him again. Two years ago me Mum died. She was 41. Me sister Elizabeth went into care and I've no idea where she is now. Me brother David's in prison for criminal assault and me brother Sean's in the Army. I've not seen either of them since they left Hulme in December 1976. Just before Christmas. The flat was boarded up and condemned unfit for human habitation when we left it. That was four years ago. It stood empty for eighteen months until a family of squatters moved in. That was 1980. I've been looking after meself since I left school and everythin fell to bits.

VOICE  Have you ever worked for a living, Fritz?

FITZ  No. I used to look for jobs. I wanted one at first so I could have some money.

VOICE  But you never quite made it. So what have you lived off — social security is it?

FITZ  For a bit. But then I got fed up with all that. All the hassles. They stopped it anyway for people like me.

VOICE  Yeh. Well I think we've got the picture. Just sit tight a

[32]

minute, Fritz.

FITZ  Oh, Jesus, Mary and Joseph.

(Blackout.)

# Seventeen

(STEPHEN and ALI in the park. Sitting close.)

ALI  Getting dark.

(STEPHEN blows on his hands.)

Yes, I know. I've been putting it off. Time to meet the gang.

STEPHEN  Just the four of you, right?

ALI  Yes. There's only Hazel you haven't seen.

STEPHEN  What should I expect?

ALI  Oh I should think you'll get along famously with her.

STEPHEN  What a disappointment. She won't lob a hand grenade at me when I walk in? Or a tin of spaghetti hoops?

ALI  No. She's more like Princess Ann than Ulrike Meinhof.

STEPHEN  Oh.

ALI  No actually, she's very nice really. When you get to know her.

STEPHEN  You mean she's appalling.

ALI  No, she's just a bit . . .

STEPHEN  Oh, great! She's one of them.

ALI  Who?

STEPHEN  Those cringing wretches you were always dragging through the door when we were at home and saying to us with horrible glee: 'But she's got this terrible personality problem', or 'I know he's smelly and offensive but there's a human being in there and anyway I've already told him he can stay a month.'

ALI  (Laughing, embarassed.) Oh, don't. No, it's not like that. Besides, I haven't got that much energy anymore.

STEPHEN  I hope that's not true. That would be a shame.

ALI  Even though I waste it all?

STEPHEN  Did I say that?

ALI  You'll get round to it.

STEPHEN  How about showing me Hulme now?

ALI  Why?

STEPHEN  I'm interested in where you've been working.

[33]

| ALI | Why? |
| STEPHEN | OK. Forget it. |
| ALI | I'll take you in a day or two, if you're still here. |
| STEPHEN | The centre closed down, didn't it? |
| ALI | That's right. So what? |
| STEPHEN | Nothing. |
| ALI | Come on. |
| STEPHEN | Nice to see you. Ali. |
| ALI | Yes. Come on. |

# Eighteen

*(Light on FITZ. He is leaning over the chair, head in hands, coughing.)*

VOICE  Don't worry, Fritz, you'll be right as rain tomorrow.
*(FITZ nods.)*
You can go now. And as long as you stay out of trouble you'll be all right. But if we pick you up again, it won't be the birch. We'll really hurt you. Pick your coat up outside. We have relieved you of your pick-axe handle. Off you go.
*(Fade.)*

# Nineteen

*(The squat. Drumming from next door. OLLY and HAZEL are both in the same sleeping bag. There are bottles of wine.)*

HAZEL  Get off. Get off. Get off. Listen. Someone's coming. Get off.
*(Enter ALI and STEPHEN.)*

OLLY  Let me go, Hazel. Let me go. Let me —. Oh.

ALI  Hi, everybody.

HAZEL  Hi. Hi.
*(OLLY waves.)*

ALI  Fitz not back? It's nearly dark.

OLLY  Been and gone.

[34]

          ALI   Where did this lot come from?
         OLLY   Who else?
          ALI   Where did he get it from?
         OLLY   Amazing, isn't he?
         OLLY   He just comes in and says 'Got this. Help yourselves.'
        HAZEL   Then he says 'I'm going up Tesco's Longsight. Anything
                you fancy?'
                So Olly of course says 'Yeh I'll have a blackcurrant
                cheesecake, please.'
          ALI   Oh, he hasn't?
         OLLY   He knows I was only joking. But have you noticed how
                fanatically loyal he is to Tesco? They should make him an
                honorary shopper. I suppose he is one.
          ALI   How long ago was this?
         OLLY   About a litre and a half. Erm . . .?
          ALI   Oh, sorry. Right. Stephen, this is —
         OLLY   Just a minute. Hazel, if you could just get off me, I'll . . .
                *(He squeezes out of the sleeping bag.)*
          ALI   This is Olly. My brother Stephen.
                *(They shake hands.)*
         OLLY   How do you do?
      STEPHEN   Fine, thanks. You?
         OLLY   In the pink.
          ALI   And this is Hazel.
      STEPHEN   Hello, Hazel.
        HAZEL   Hello, Stephen.
         OLLY   You must excuse Hazel, Stephen. She's a bit loathe to
                stand up and say hello on account of how she hasn't got
                any knickers on at the moment.
        HAZEL   It's only my jeans I haven't got on.
      STEPHEN   I'm sorry if we interrupted you.
         OLLY   Not at all.
        HAZEL   I was just mending my jeans and I thought I'd sit in my
                sleeping bag because it's a bit cold because the heating
                only came on half an hour ago.
         OLLY   We shouldn't have been doing it in here anyway. This is
                the communal room. For when we do it communally.
          ALI   What's going on next door?
         OLLY   Eh?
          ALI   The drumming. What's it in aid of?
         OLLY   What? I can't hear you because of all that fucking
                drumming. Shut up!
                [35]

*(Silence.)*

HAZEL   Now why didn't we think of that before?
*(The drumming starts again.)*

OLLY   They're having a party.

HAZEL   I think it's going to be noisy because it's apparently a house-cooling, not that these houses need it. Be nice and quiet when they've gone though.

OLLY   According to Fitz, they've got a steel band coming later. It's going to be a riot.

ALI   How does he know?

OLLY   He went and asked. In fact I think that's where the er . . .
*(He is pouring out wine into plastic cups.)*
Would you like to start catching up?

HAZEL   We didn't even know Ali had a brother until yesterday. Except Fitz. Ali says you studied politics and economics.

STEPHEN   That's right. I've been working in a London housing department. Till January.

HAZEL   Get the sack?

STEPHEN   Yep.

HAZEL   I'd really like to hear about it.

STEPHEN   Well . . .

ALI   Oh don't get him started on that.

OLLY   Oh come off it, we want the goods straight from the horse's mouth. I mean is it or is it not true that 26% of all homes in England and Wales still have outside toilets but only 58% of these are operable at any one time the remainder being clogged up with housing officials doing surveys about how many homes in England and Wales have outside toilets?

STEPHEN   I wouldn't know.

HAZEL   Let's have a toast.

OLLY   Right. You give us it.

HAZEL   Oh, I can't think of anything.

OLLY   Come on.

HAZEL   I've thought of one.

OLLY   Ladies and gentlemen, raise your glasses, please. The toast is:

HAZEL   Thank God the electricity's back on.
*(The lights go out. Drums stop.)*

OLLY   Yes, well done, Hazel.

[36]

# Twenty

(*Fade up sound of steel band and noises of party. Lights up on the squat. Later that evening. OLLY, ALI, HAZEL, STEPHEN and FITZ are drinking. OLLY is currently talking over the noise from next door.*)

OLLY   They had a terrific sense of humour some of these guys. That's something you never expect. Beautifully sardonic, you know. Terrific piss-takers. One guy, was one of the guides, I used to spend a lot of time with him on trips, his name, believe it or not, talking about a sense of humour, was 'canoe-penis', and this particular time I'm thinking of we were —

(*The others have erupted into hoots of laughter.*)

What's the matter? What did I say?

HAZEL   Canoe-penis?

ALI   You liar, Olly.

OLLY   I'm telling you his name was canoe-penis. What's so funny about that?

HAZEL   Why was he called that?

(*More mirth.*)

OLLY   Well it wasn't because his canoe was a funny shape. So look, listen, I'm trying to tell you, there was this one particular time we were heading up river in our canoe —

(*Howls of laughter.*)

Oh fuck it. Gimme some more wine. What's the matter with him?

(*FITZ is holding his sides and laughing.*)

ALI   I think he's hurt himself with laughing.

OLLY   Oy. Fitz.

FITZ   When I was a kid at school we had this gym master and we used to call him . . . we used to call him . . .

(*He dissolves into laughter.*)

ALI   What?

OLLY   He's not going to make it. Where were you all afternoon anyway?

(*FITZ is still laughing.*)

|  | I wish I hadn't mentioned it. Why did I mention it anyway? What was I talking about? |
|---|---|
| HAZEL | You weren't talking about anything, you were interrupting me. |
| OLLY | What were you talking about? |
| HAZEL | I was agreeing with Stephen. I think we ought to start organizing a campaign in this area so we don't end up like in Hulme. |
| OLLY | Oh, yeh. Wine, wine, gimme wine, I gotta have it. |
| ALI | Anybody else? |
| HAZEL | Yes please. Stephen, do you? I only want a little bit, Ali. |
| ALI | Fitz? |
| FITZ | Yeh. |
| ALI | I think you're pissed. |
| HAZEL | Don't you think, Ali? |
| ALI | I don't know. I suppose I do, yeh. |
| OLLY | Didn't do them much good in Hulme. It really grows on you, doesn't it? I hope they go on all night now cos if they stop I'd never be able to sleep. |
| HAZEL | I think we really ought to. I've always thought it would be a good idea if we could organize ourselves more in smaller groups. Haven't I, Oll? |
| OLLY | Anybody know where they're going next door? |
| FITZ | They've found a squat in Chorlton. |
| OLLY | Chorlton? Snobs. |
| FITZ | Must go for a slash. |
|  | *(Exit FITZ.)* |
| OLLY | That's his third. |
| ALI | Well, it's a party. |
| OLLY | Quite right. But I want him up at the crack of dawn pinching handkerchiefs and pocketwatches. |
| HAZEL | Maybe you could stay a while and help us to get it going. |
| STEPHEN | I've got other plans, I'm afraid. |
| HAZEL | Do you think we should elect local leaders to represent us? Would that help? |
| STEPHEN | Up to a point, yes. |
| OLLY | So long as nobody gets the chance to decide anything important you mean. Mas vino, por favor. |
| STEPHEN | That's not what I meant actually. |
| OLLY | I think it's a mistake this business of having leaders. The |

[38]

next time some bastard comes along and personally I'm expecting one any minute and says he's going to solve all the problems, I vote we shoot him immediately. Actually, that's a bit crude. The Zuni Indians in New Mexico have got the perfect antidote to leaders.

*(HAZEL groans.)*

They realised years ago that the last thing any sensible person wants is more leaders. What we need in fact is less leaders. So what they do is this: any Indian showing signs of what we would call natural authority, anybody expressing a desire to be a leader or even looking like they might turn into one, they hang them up by their thumbs till they confess.

ALI To what?

OLLY Anything. Doesn't matter. The important thing is to hang the buggers up by their thumbs. Witchcraft usually. Stephen here wouldn't last five minutes.

*(he looks at STEPHEN's thumbs. Enter FITZ.)*

Never been to New Mexico, have you?

STEPHEN No. Have you?

OLLY Fraid not. I get all my best stuff out of books.

FITZ He's been to Brazil though, haven't you, Olly?

HAZEL You see, Steve, the problem with Olly is he gets so pissed he doesn't know what he's talking about.

OLLY That's not strictly true. The problem is I can't get pissed often enough.

ALI What's the world coming to? Have some more wine.

HAZEL Just a minute, just a minute, before you change the subject. What do these wonderful smart idyllic Indians have instead of leaders?

*(ALI is serving more wine.)*

OLLY Urine drip? Piles? Leprosy? I give up.

HAZEL Come on, smart arse, what do they do when things go wrong? Who sorts it out? I think Stephen would be interested.

OLLY Quite simple. They have a shaman.

HAZEL What's he when he's at home?

OLLY He or she is someone who's in touch with spirits.

HAZEL You might've known it would be something cruddy like that.

FITZ They're not cruddy, they're supernatural. They've got like magic powers, haven't they, Oll?

OLLY  Certainly have.

FITZ  Medicine men.

HAZEL  What you talking about, Fitz? If you listen to him he'll fill your head full of junk.

ALI  But is this person a real person, a member of the tribe?

OLLY  Oh yeh, I mean they live in the village usually.

HAZEL  Well how come they're supernatural? I mean how do they get their powers?

OLLY  Well, you see, Hazel, once every four years they have this primitive ritual they call 'localgovermentelekshun' and they have magic pieces of paper that go into magic boxes with secret inscriptions on them that nobody can understand except the Indians who work on the TV.

STEPHEN  Isn't the shaman usually the most unstable member of the community — what we would call a mental defective or a person perhaps with a severe personality disorder?

OLLY  That's right. They'd hang our leaders up by the thumbs, we'd put theirs into a mental home.

ALI  What do you mean by unstable? How unstable?

OLLY  Well a shaman will usually have begun having what we'd call cataleptic fits during childhood and adolescence. Foaming at the mouth, injuring themselves and what have you. This may be what singles a shaman out initially. This violent withdrawal from consciousness. Later in order to achieve the same state of removed consciousness a lot of tribes use drugs or alcohol to induce a trance. What they call 'getting religious'. Then if you're a real shaman you'll see spirits, visions, you'll be in touch with the souls of the dead who'll help you with advice. It's a very powerful vocation but it has its drawbacks. Being in contact with the souls of the dead signifies being dead oneself.

FITZ  I'm religious as a newt.

OLLY  Course you don't need dope or booze to be a shaman. Your visions might well occur in dreams or even while you're wide awake. As long as you're receptive. That's the mark of a real top class shaman. If he's really shit hot he might be able to persuade a powerful spirit to return to the world and solve your problems for you.

HAZEL  If only they'd tried all this in Hulme.

OLLY  Right. You see, the real problem with that place is it's infested.

[40]

ALI     You can say that again.

OLLY    Not just rats and cockroaches though. Ghosts.

HAZEL   Oh, Jesus.

OLLY    The people, the buildings, the rats, the cockroaches are all infested with ghosts. They're haunted by the wandering spirits of all the departed bastards who tried to organize the place.

        *(FITZ is laughing.)*

        Architects, designers, town planners, politicians, bureaucrats, policemen, councillors —

ALI     Community workers.

OLLY    —community workers, thank you very much, probation officers, lawyers, housing officials, water board officials, gas board officials, electricity board officials —

FITZ    Right.

OLLY    They're a curse. The lot of them.

FITZ    Right.

OLLY    A blight. What we need is a powerful spirit to drive them out.

FITZ    Right.

HAZEL   How come we always end up talking about garbage? We were having a serious discussion.

ALI     No we weren't — we were having a party.

HAZEL   No, Ali, Stephen was making a serious point, I think. Weren't you, Stephen?

STEPHEN  I can't remember.

        *(OLLY sits stock still with his eyes glazed over.)*

FITZ    Hey, Oll?

HAZEL   Just ignore him. He's smashed out of his head.

ALI     What's he doing?

FITZ    He's goin into a trance.

HAZEL   Oh, Christ. Olly, stop pissing about, you've made a big enough exhibition of yourself already. Oh, just ignore him. He's such a bloody idiot.

ALI     More wine anybody? There's a bit left.

        *(They all have wine.)*

        More wine, Olly?

        *(No response.)*

FITZ    See? He must be in a trance.

HAZEL   He must be dead.

ALI     OK, Stephen?

STEPHEN  I'm fine.

        [41]

(*Silence for a second then ALI starts giggling.*

Yeh, I know it's funny, and I don't want to look like a spoilsport either, but, you know . . . I mean: out there — real problems, bad problems, for real people. And they can be put right even now, but only by people facing up and working together. And . . . you know . . . we all like a bit of fun, but to talk about all that and at the same time this kind of thing, I find . . . you know . . .

ALI     Yeh. But it's not very often we have much fun. You have to sometimes.

STEPHEN     Oh, shit.

(*The steel band has stopped next door but we can still hear talking, laughter.*

ALI     Where *were* you all afternoon then?

(*OLLY gets to his feet slowly, his eyes staring.*)

OLLY     Javaritu. Javaritu. Yes, it's me. Olliero. Javaritu. Old friend. I need your spirit here. Can't you come for just a little while? We really need you. Javaritu?

(*He suddenly snaps out of it.*)

No. Says he's too busy.

(*FITZ and ALI amused. Even HAZEL is a little bit amused.*)

You bastards, you've hogged all the wine.

HAZEL     Who were you talking to then?

OLLY     Javaritu.

HAZEL     And who's Javaritu?

OLLY     Canoe-penis. Told you he had a great sense of humour.

STEPHEN     He's dead then?

OLLY     As a dodo.

HAZEL     How do you know that?

ALI     You're making it up.

FITZ     He was there.

OLLY     Someone stuck a spear in him.

(*The music recommences loudly.*)

HAZEL     What?

OLLY     What?

HAZEL     What?

OLLY     What?

HAZEL     What did you say?

OLLY     When?

HAZEL     What?

OLLY     This could go on all night.

(*Blackout. Fade music.*)

[42]

# Twenty one

*(The squat. The next morning. OLLY and HAZEL are curled up asleep together as are FITZ and ALI. STEPHEN is awake and looking at ALI. From next door the noise of hammering and tearing. HAZEL wakes up.)*

HAZEL    What's going on? What time is it?

STEPHEN    Nine o'clock.

HAZEL    It's freezing. Have you had any sleep?
*(He shakes his head.)*
What's going on?

STEPHEN    The party finished about seven then your neighbours moved out as soon as it was light. The place was empty for exactly twelve minutes. Then they arrived and started smashing the place up.

HAZEL    Who?

STEPHEN    I don't know. Whoever it is is making a good job of it. Landlord maybe.

HAZEL    Choice, isn't it?
*(She disappears back into her sleeping bag. Fade.)*


INTERVAL


# Twenty two

*(October. The squat. FITZ sits reading in his overcoat. HAZEL writing a letter. FITZ apparently having difficulty.)*

HAZEL    Do you want me to help you, Fitz?
*(He shows her the word.)*
That one? Oh bloody hell. Hermetically.

FITZ    Hermetically. What does it mean?

HAZEL    It means, I think, that it's air-tight. What is this? One of Olly's?

[43]

FITZ    Yeh.

        *(He goes back to reading.)*

HAZEL   I'm writing a letter. Trouble is they take so bloody long to get there. You know, Fitz, if you wanted to write to your brothers or anything I could give you a hand. If you need it. If Ali was busy.

FITZ    It's all right, thanks.

HAZEL   Hazel.

FITZ    Hazel. I haven't got any address anyway, so . . .

        *(He goes back to reading, she to writing. Enter OLLY straight into a sleeping bag.)*

OLLY    Hi. Hi.

FITZ    Hi, Olly. What's that?

        *(He shows him the book.)*

OLLY    It's got an air-tight seal on it. It's fused.

HAZEL   Did you get it then?

OLLY    No.

FITZ    What?

OLLY    Job as a porter in a hospital. I've done it before so I thought I might get it. Bit of bread.

FITZ    What hospital?

OLLY    Doesn't matter, does it?

HAZEL   What did they say?

OLLY    Nothing. There were a hundred and fifty million other people in front of me in the queue. Some of the poor sods had camped out. In this weather, I ask you.

HAZEL   Never mind those poor sods, what about you, poor sod? O, Olly, are you disappointed? Would you like a cup of tea?

OLLY    There must be a catch. Is the gas on?

HAZEL   Yes.

OLLY    Water?

HAZEL   No. But I filled a kettle last night and we've still got some left.

OLLY    Great. Where'd you nick the tea from?

HAZEL   He didn't nick it, I bought it.

OLLY    Oh. Had a letter?

HAZEL   *(Going out.)* Yeh. It's there. You can read it.

OLLY    No thanks. How you doing, Fitz old son?

FITZ    Cold. I'm seein a bloke this afternoon who thinks he knows where we can lift some coal somewhere in Trafford Park.

OLLY    That would be ace. Watch yourself though.

FITZ    Pity about the job.

        [44]

OLLY    Fuck it. I'm too old to work. Where's Ali?

FITZ    Gone into Hulme.

OLLY    With Stephen?

*(FITZ nods.)*

Don't worry, he'll piss off soon.

FITZ    Yeh. None of my business anyway.

OLLY    No, no. Nor mine.

*(He picks up the letter and skims through.)*

'Dear Hazel' blah, blah, blah, 'your uncle Terence says we're in for a cold winter'. How does he know? Blah, blah. 'Your letters seem very vague about what your plans are.' Blah. 'We're both looking forward to meeting Kenneth.' Who? Oh, me. Fucking liars. 'Try to understand our concern.' Blah. blah. 'We can't go on sending money indefinitely without some idea of what your plans are.' Blah, blah, blah. Your ever loving parents, Adolf and Eva.' *(Blackout.)*

# Twenty three

*(The road bridge. ALI and STEPHEN looking out.)*

STEPHEN    You're catching a cold. Here.

*(He hands her a handkerchief.)*

ALI    Thanks. Is it all right if I blow on it?

STEPHEN    How long since you were here?

ALI    The day you came. It's always a little bit worse each time. There are quite a few more empty flats.

STEPHEN    What about those people you couldn't find?

ALI    In the past some have turned up again back in Hulme or down near us. But most of them I lose track of. They must go somewhere. Relatives or friends. Somewhere.

STEPHEN    I didn't realise things had gone this far.

ALI    *(Pointing.)* Look. Look at that.

STEPHEN    Who does it? Kids?

ALI    It's mainly kids. They drag an old sofa into an empty room and set fire to it. Then when the fire brigade comes they throw half-bricks at them. The fire station's only over there — you can almost see it.

STEPHEN    Don't you get fed up?

[45]

ALI Yes.

STEPHEN Does Fitz ever come with you?

ALI No. He lived in Hulme for five years. He never comes back unless he has to.

STEPHEN He doesn't spend much time at the house.

ALI No. He's travelling a lot further afield, taking a lot more care recently. Also, he's been trying to keep out of your way.

STEPHEN Sorry.

ALI Don't apologise to me. He keeps pretty busy anyway. I shouldn't worry.

STEPHEN Doing what exactly?

ALI Oh, don't be so pompous. What do you think he does? What do you expect him to do? Starve to death? Get a job? Join the young Liberals?

STEPHEN I was only asking a simple question.

ALI That'll be the day. I'll be in the same boat soon. I'm nearly broke. Maybe Hazel and I should go on the game. Jesus, they're taking their time.

STEPHEN Olly would make a very good ponce.

ALI I expect you loathe him.

STEPHEN No, I like him. He reminds me of me.

ALI You joking?

STEPHEN No.

ALI Full marks. I didn't think you'd see that.
*(Stephen winks.)*

STEPHEN With certain crucial distinctions, of course.

ALI Of course. He only pretends to be a phoney. You're the real thing.

STEPHEN That's right.

ALI Here they come.
*(A fire engine passes underneath them.)*

STEPHEN Are you having it off with him?

ALI No.

STEPHEN Have you ever?

ALI No.
*(Pause.)*

STEPHEN You're not having it off with Fitz, are you?

ALI What if I am?

STEPHEN Nothing. Just wanted to know.

ALI *(Laughing.)* Oh, yeh. Just wanted to know.

STEPHEN Well?

[46]

ALI He's got a crush on me. I'm very fond of him.

STEPHEN It must be very tempting then.

ALI You've got a bloody nerve, you really have.

*(Pause.)*

STEPHEN Dad and Catherine leave in three weeks.

ALI Yeh.

STEPHEN It's not long.

ALI No.

STEPHEN I said I'd ring by today to let them know what's happening.

ALI Yeh.

STEPHEN Frankly, I think what you're doing is laudable but useless.

ALI Of course you do.

STEPHEN You're swanning about like some Florence Nightingale bringing nothing but compassion to people who've disappeared by the time you call again. It's a waste of a valuable resource. You're squandering yourself. And for what? What do you think you're going to achieve?

ALI Nothing. I didn't come here to achieve anything.

STEPHEN Look. I want you to come to London and live with me. We'll work together. It's not as bad as this and it won't be if people are prepared to fight.

ALI Why don't you stay here with me and fight?

STEPHEN I've never seen anything like this. Nobody's looking for the answers anymore.

ALI All the more reason for people to stay.

STEPHEN Look, you're not fighting—you're mopping up. There's nothing you can do that will make that place any better tomorrow than it was yesterday. Face it. It's a write-off.

ALI Oh, that's great. You really haven't changed. Sorry, you lot, you're a write-off.

STEPHEN Oh, for Christ's sake, Ali, wake up. You haven't got a corner in concern.

ALI I didn't say I had.

STEPHEN You've rammed it down my throat for three days. It isn't enough to have your heart in the right place. What really fucks me up is that you could be contributing instead of hiding away in this dustbin, inflating your own ego. Get out of this place. Get away from those people. They're going nowhere.

ALI Oh, piss off back to London. Get back to your cronies and start building a beautiful tomorrow if you really think you've got the answers. But for Christ's sake ask them not

[47]

to make any more mistakes like last time because some of
us are still up to our noses in the shit.
(Pause.)

STEPHEN You've stayed here too long. With the wrong people.

ALI Look, don't patronise me, please.

STEPHEN People like Olly live off people like you. He's dead weight.
He's a running joke at his own expense. Completely self-
absorbed. He *wants* everything to disintegrate.

ALI Why?

STEPHEN Why what?

ALI Why do you think he wants that?

STEPHEN I don't know. I don't care.

ALI That's it. You really don't. That's the difference. We're just
going round in the same old circle we used to, and I'd like
to stop it *now*, please.

STEPHEN Why did you leave home?

ALI Oh, Jesus.

STEPHEN I thought it was because you thought we were going to
bully you into the kind of life you didn't want. But we
wouldn't have. You wouldn't have let us.

ALI No.

STEPHEN So?

ALI You haven't got a clue, have you?

STEPHEN Catherine? Nobody gets along with Catherine. Do you
think he shouldn't have remarried? Is that what—?

ALI It wasn't Catherine, it was us. It wasn't why should I leave,
it was why should I stay. Why do you think she was an
alcoholic?

STEPHEN Oh, come on . . .

ALI If he wanted another wife, why did he have to pick a
woman who couldn't win an argument with a chair leg? I
lived with her for four year and none of us knew the first
thing about her. There wasn't really a place for her in our
home. Why wasn't there? Why couldn't we make one?
Why did I leave home? It wasn't a home, it was an asylum.
With you two talking non-stop about the new society and
social priorities, and her upstairs swallowing vodka and
pills because she felt lonely and stupid . . .

STEPHEN You won't pay her back by staying here.

ALI I'm not trying to pay her back. You're just never going to
understand, are you?
(Pause.)

[48]

STEPHEN  What shall I tell the old man then?

ALI  Tell him we'll be there.

STEPHEN  We better leave today.

# Twenty four

*(The squat. ALI, STEPHEN, OLLY, HAZEL, and FITZ.)*

ALI  I expect I'll be away for about a month.
*(FITZ is looking at ALI and then at STEPHEN.)*
I might not get a chance to see him again, you see.

FITZ  When?

ALI  We might as well go straightaway. Not much to pack. We'll be hitching.

HAZEL  Scotland, isn't it?

STEPHEN  Yeh.

OLLY  I wonder if the water's come back on.

HAZEL  Oh yeh.

FITZ  It hasn't.

OLLY  We'll just check.
*(Exeunt HAZEL and OLLY.)*

STEPHEN  I'll wait outside. Will we be going immediately, Ali?

ALI  Yes.

STEPHEN  Goodbye then, Fitz.
*(Exit STEPHEN.)*

ALI  I need a few days away anyway, Fitz. When I come back I'll have sorted a lot of things out in my head. OK? Fitz? Take care while I'm gone then. Make Olly fend for himself a bit more. I'll probably have some money, that'll be good, eh? About a month then, Fitz. I'll bring you a birthday present.
*(Exit ALI. Fade.)*

# Twenty five

*(November.*

*The squat. The chairs have gone. HAZEL is mending gloves. OLLY is in his sleeping bag, reading. FITZ is sitting. All three look tired.)*

HAZEL  Is there any mending you need doing, Fitz, while I'm busy? Anything you need doing?

FITZ  It's all right, thanks.

HAZEL  I wouldn't mind. I'd be pleased to do it in fact. If you've got anything.

*(FITZ thinks for quite a long time.)*

I mean, if you haven't got anything, that's OK.

FITZ  I haven't got anything.

HAZEL  That's fine then.

*(Silence.)*

It's incredible how much colder it is when you haven't got any heat.

OLLY  Never occurred to me before.

HAZEL  You know what I mean. When you've got some heat you take it for granted. You don't stop to think how cold it actually is. Would be, rather. Without it. If some bugger somewhere would just flick a switch.

OLLY  Think I'll write to my MP about it. Second thoughts, I think I'll complain to one of the new completely-unofficial nothing-to-do-with-us-honestly spontaneously-constituted entirely-local civilian peace keeping patrols. Before they started keeping the peace in Hulme there was the odd fire. Now every night's Guy Fawkes' night. They've certainly cleaned up the streets. Nobody's got time to commit crimes anymore — they're all at home boarding up their windows.

*(FITZ is putting gloves on.)*

Going out?

FITZ  I'll see if I can scrounge some wood or somethin.

HAZEL  Oh, Fitz, I didn't mean that.

FITZ  It's all right. I'd rather be outside for a bit anyway.

[50]

*(From next door the noise of footsteps, crashing and laughter.)*

FITZ  Shit. I thought I heard them coming in in the night.

HAZEL  Who would live in there now?

FITZ  Pissheads, dossers, scum, fucking loonies. They don't know what they're at half the time.
*(More crashing and yelling.)*

OLLY  Oh, great.

FITZ  We'll have to be careful from now on else they'll be in here. From now on we shouldn't leave the house empty ever. Right?

OLLY  Yeh. OK, Fitz. Hazel.

HAZEL  Yeh.
*(FITZ picks up a heavy cane, puts it in his pocket and goes out.)*

OLLY  What's the matter?

HAZEL  Well I don't know . . . I just don't know what he wants from me. It's like talking to yourself.

OLLY  He doesn't want anything from you. Forget all that. It just embarrasses him.

HAZEL  Well are we supposed to avoid talking about Ali or not? Is he upset or what? I'd just like to know what I can and can't say. Only sometimes the atmosphere's like ice and I honestly feel as if he's about to whack me with that stick. And does he really need to sit with it across his lap?

OLLY  Why are you asking me?

HAZEL  Hell, Olly, we've lived here for four months and I'm never going to get to know that kid.

OLLY  Well you'll just have to try a bit harder, won't you?

HAZEL  Oh, you really sicken me sometimes.

OLLY  If you don't mind shutting your face, Hazel, I was reading.

HAZEL  *(Knocking it out of his hands.)* Sod the book.

OLLY  Oh . . .!
*(From next door a lot of laughing, screaming, banging and jumping up and down. It goes on so long that they cannot continue. OLLY zips himself into his sleeping bag and disappears. Eventually it stops. HAZEL kicks the bag.)*

HAZEL  Olly. Olly.
*(He appears.)*

OLLY  What?

HAZEL  There's no chance of the university finding us grants now is there?

[51]

OLLY  Not until after Christmas anyway.

HAZEL  Do you think we could find jobs if we tried a bit more?

OLLY  Like where?

HAZEL  What are we doing here then? Are we waiting for something? Is it all suddenly going to get better?

OLLY  Doubt it.

HAZEL  Then why don't we go somewhere else? Why do we have to stay here?

OLLY  We live here, that's why.

HAZEL  Well could we at least use our own bedroom again instead of the three of us down here?

OLLY  When we get some electricity back on or some coal, yes.
*(He zips himself up again.)*

HAZEL  I wrote to Mum and Dad again yesterday. I said we might like to spend Christmas with them. I don't know whether they'd have us.
*(He unzips slowly.)*

OLLY  Hazel. Let's get this crystal clear for the very last time. Wild horses wouldn't get me to spend Christmas with your parents. I'd hate to spend Christmas with your parents. In fact, I don't ever want to meet your parents ever. Ever. Got it?

HAZEL  Yes, Olly, I think I did.
*(Sound of breaking glass.)*
Oh Jesus, what was that?

OLLY  Next door.

HAZEL  *(On her feet.)* No, I don't think so. Oh, God.

OLLY  *(Getting out of the bag.)* Well what do you think it was?
*(Enter FITZ.)*

FITZ  The house at the far end's on fire.
*(Exit FITZ followed by HAZEL and OLLY.)*

# Twenty six

*(OLLY, FITZ and HAZEL watching the fire in the street.)*

HAZEL  Oh, God, it's like a bonfire already.

FITZ  Don't go any closer.

OLLY  Where's the fire brigade then?

HAZEL  Is there anybody in, do we know?

[52]

FITZ  Three kids they think. Their mothers usually leave them to
go out to work. Nobody's come out so far.

OLLY  Well nobody'll come out now.
*(They watch in silence.)*

FITZ  See you back home.
*(Exit FITZ.)*

HAZEL  What do you think happened? It was glass breaking wasn't
it?

OLLY  Looks like it's our turn to be protected.
*(Fade.)*


# Twenty seven

*(On the bridge. OLLY and FITZ. FITZ looking about him
uncertainly.)*

OLLY  Where to?

FITZ  *(Shaking his head.)* Those two were the main two blokes
for anything like coal or any kind of heavy stuff like that.

OLLY  Do you think they've been arrested or what?

FITZ  Well they could've been but, see, they didn't leave Hulme
much themselves. Other people did most of the work. And
the cops don't go in. So I'm thinkin maybe their own
people got sick of them. They were both bastards. Or the
peace keepers got them. Or they just decided to get out
while they still could. Whatever happened that's this place
more or less finished. Look. Those blocks are more or less
empty. They've concentrated themselves in those two.
That one and that one. I dunno if you noticed. Not many
people about but them we did see was mainly youngish
blokes.

OLLY  You think the families have all gone?

FITZ  That's what I'm thinkin. But there was nobody there I
know anymore so I don't know how I can find out what's
goin on. I don't want to know. There's nothin here for me
now.

OLLY  Why those two blocks?

FITZ  Well if I wanted to defend meself that's where I'd go.
They've only got those front doors. There's nothing at the
back. They're not overlooked by taller blocks. You can't

[53]

get underneath them and there's no deck access.

OLLY  Defend yourself against what?

FITZ  Anything.

OLLY  Do you think they've got weapons?

FITZ  Some of them are sure to have shooters.

OLLY  Nothing else though — nothing bigger?

FITZ  No. Don't think so.

OLLY  Not having any coal doesn't seem like such a problem. Shall we go back through the park?

*(Fade.)*

# Twenty eight

*(In the park. OLLY and FITZ sit on the bench.)*

OLLY  You know, Fitz, you don't look so hot. You should take it easy a bit. You don't have to go prowlin around all the time. Stay at home. Get some kip.

*(FITZ nods.)*

FITZ  Wish we could go to Southport again.

OLLY  Christ, yes, I'd forgotten that.

FITZ  I think about it all the time.

OLLY  Do you know that was . . . that was only three months ago? I remember now. You had a great time, didn't you? We all did.

FITZ  Best day I've had for ages.

OLLY  We'll go again. Next summer. Easter. I'll get another jalopy. Is it a date?

FITZ  Yeh.

*(Silence.)*

OLLY  Mind you, looks like it could be just me and you. And Ali.

FITZ  What about Hazel?

OLLY  I think not. I reckon she'll be off soon.

*(FITZ looks a bit confused.)*

What? What do you want to ask?

FITZ  Nothin.

OLLY  Noticed anything?

FITZ  What?

OLLY  The lake.

*(FITZ shakes his head.)*

[54]

No ducks. How do you like that, eh?

FITZ   I should've thought of that.

OLLY   You're slipping. Mind you, take a long time to roast one on a candle.

FITZ   Bloke tried to flog me a campin gaz thing the other day. He wanted too much. Told him to get knotted. Well, we got some wood anyway.

OLLY   Did we?

*(FITZ stands up and takes one end of the bench. OLLY takes the other.*

*Exeunt carrying the bench. Fade.)*


# Twenty nine

*(The squat. Empty. Enter OLLY and FITZ with the bench. Singing from next door.)*

OLLY   She must be upstairs.

*(He goes out.)*

Hazel? Are you there?

*(He comes in.)*

She's gone out. Oh, bloody hell.

*(Door slam. Enter HAZEL. She seems to be dazed. She sits.)*

OLLY   We told you not to leave the place empty! You knew we were out, you stupid bitch! Do you want those fucking loonies in here? for shit's sake, what's the matter with you? *(OLLY is shaking with anger.)*

HAZEL   A bloke came looking for Fitz. He said Fitz owed him some money for a camping gaz.

OLLY   You didn't let him in?

HAZEL   He said he knew Fitz. He said I'd have to give him some money. I said he'd have to see Fitz. So he punched me in the face and banged my head against the wall. He said he'd smash the place up and me with it if I didn't give him some money. I had two quid left from what Mum sent last week so I gave him it. He punched me in the stomach. But I didn't have any more to give him. When he went I didn't want to stay here so I went for a walk. I thought I might meet you.

[55]

FITZ He must've been watching the house.
  *(OLLY sits on the bench.)*
OLLY I mean we're going to have to board the place up if you go
  letting people in the front door. For shit's sake, Hazel.
  *(Yells and crashing from next door.)*
HAZEL *(Crying.)* I've decided, Olly. As soon as some money
  comes, I'm going. I can't stand it.
  *(She cries. OLLY sits at the opposite end of the bench.)*
FITZ I've had enough of those pissheads.
  *(Exit FITZ with his cane. Blackout.)*

# Thirty

*(The squat. A car sounding its horn insistently outside.
Some carrier bags filled with clothes are on the floor. OLLY
alone. Enter HAZEL with some small items which she
shoves into a bag. Enter FITZ.)*

FITZ It is your taxi. He says he won't wait.
HAZEL Make him wait just half a minute, Fitz, please.
  *(Exit FITZ. HAZEL kisses OLLY and gives him a piece of
  paper and money.)*
HAZEL I don't need this. This is the address and number. If you do
  want to change your mind or if you want to call me.
OLLY Fine. Thanks, Hazel.
HAZEL I'll have to go.
OLLY You were lucky to get a taxi to come at all. .
HAZEL OK. I'll see you after Christmas then, Oll. OK?
OLLY Yeh.
HAZEL OK, then.
  *(The horn sounds impatiently.)*
  Try and take care of yourself then.
  *(Enter FITZ.)*
FITZ He's going now, he says.
HAZEL All right.
  *(She snatches up her bags and has a quick look round and
  rushes out. FITZ carries one of her bags for her.)*
HAZEL *(As she goes.)* See you, Oll.
OLLY See you, Hazel.
  *(Door slams. Enter FITZ. Fade.)*
  [56]

# Thirty one

*(The squat. OLLY alone sitting on the bench thinking. A key in the door.)*

OLLY  Fitz?

*(Door closes. Enter STEPHEN.)*

STEPHEN  Hello.

OLLY  Hello, Stephen.

*(He looks behind Stephen.)*

STEPHEN  Place looks rough.

OLLY  You bet.

STEPHEN  What's been happening?

OLLY  Fires, fighting, arrests. Nothing serious. Somebody organized some peace-keeping vigilantes. Philanthropists to a man.

STEPHEN  I'd like to leave a letter for Fitz. I want to pick up a few things for Ali and myself if you don't mind.

OLLY  No.

STEPHEN  Do you have any power now?

OLLY  Occasionally someone slips up and we get electricity for an hour or two. This is yours.

*(There is a thermos flask on the floor.)*

OLLY  Would you care for a cup of tea?

STEPHEN  That's very decent of you.

*(He sits. OLLY pours him some tea.)*

OLLY  Where is she?

STEPHEN  She travelled straight to London with Dad and Catherine. They fly out tomorrow. Ali wanted to say hello to some friends. Too good an opportunity.

OLLY  She's coming back then?

STEPHEN  I think so, yes.

OLLY  You couldn't talk her out of it?

STEPHEN  There's still time. *(Drinking up.)* Can I leave this with you?

*(He offers a letter and a small package.)*

OLLY  He'll be back anytime. It's getting dark. Finish the tea and you can have your flask back.

STEPHEN  I brought some blankets for you.

[57]

OLLY  Thanks.

STEPHEN  From Ali.

OLLY  Fitz has decided we'll have to leave here soon. He's looking for a new place now. I fancy Wilmslow myself but Fitz thinks Cheadle Hulme's the place to be these days.

STEPHEN  Very quiet next door.

OLLY  We did have some new neighbours but Fitz couldn't get along with them. Street's practically empty.

STEPHEN  I noticed.

OLLY  Amazing what a few well-worded handbills will do when they're backed up with half-bricks and the odd can of petrol. Fitz is right. Won't be long now. They're just waiting for the right moment to come and persuade the rest of us in the street of our democratic right to piss off somewhere else.

STEPHEN  Well. So long as you're happy.

OLLY  This is it.

STEPHEN  I think I will go now.

OLLY  You know, if you're really worried about Ali coming back to Fitz, there's no need, in my opinion.

STEPHEN  You can keep the flask.

OLLY  Off hand I can't think of a safer place for her in view of what's coming. She'll be much better off in the long run with Fitz here than with you in London. He's been training since he was nine.

STEPHEN  And what is coming?

OLLY  I can't predict the grisly details but we both know there's a hard time ahead.

STEPHEN  But Fitz will survive it.

OLLY  I would say he has a good chance. He's been given the right mental equipment. He knows exactly what he's up against from experience. I think it's very clear in his head which is why he doesn't say anything about it. For ten years he's lived as an outsider. That's what he was given. He spent his boyhood at the back of every queue till he learned that everybody he met was going to rip him off or slap him down. People like Fitz are only nominally part of the same society as the rest of us. Most of them only exist for us as 'problems' or 'victims' of 'political failure'. That's what we decide to call them to set them apart. It's interesting. Other, 'primitive' societies draw much cleaner

[58]

distinctions. It's one of the earliest, most human, most basic distinctions: between me, my small group, and the outsiders. It's so sharp with some people that their words for themselves — 'Kiowa', for example, or 'Zuni' in fact — are also their words for 'human beings'. Outsiders are not just failures or victims or even dirty foreigners or enemies. They aren't human beings at all.

STEPHEN What's this got to do with Fitz?

OLLY Only that I sometimes think that he senses a similar distinction or something very like it. Between himself, those people he knows personally, and everybody else. In Brazil it was the most frightening thing about meeting Indians in the remote parts of the forests. Those who'd had little or no contact with civilizados. Their eyes would have a completely flat, expressionless look. They follow your movements without registering that you are human like them. It doesn't occur to them that you have a right to life. You're a piece of meat. They live in a little hole cut in the jungle. It contains their moral scheme. Everything outside that is fair game. They'd kill a parrot for its feathers and a white man for his rifle without seeing any distinction.

STEPHEN That's what civilizing means. Not transistor radios and plastic cups or even medicine. Extending their boundaries to include other men. Seeing other people as the same as yourself.

OLLY And caring about people as people.

STEPHEN Sure.

OLLY And being reluctant to harm them.

STEPHEN Right.

OLLY Then how the fuck do you explain all this?

STEPHEN You see, this noble savage stuff is fine. They form a clearing in the jungle, or they build a circle of huts in the desert, and of course they can organize it so everybody can live the way they'd like — there are probably only about two dozen of them. When you've got sixty millions . . .

OLLY What? Sombody has to be at the back of the queue? A certain percentage inevitably gets the chop? What is it then — natural selection? What percentage? 5%? 20%? That doesn't cut much ice with the likes of Fitz. What happens to caring and being reluctant to harm? If we did those things would it really matter how many of us there were?

[59]

You can't just say it's priorities when it's this extreme. It's whether we really care. We had the money, the resources, the knowledge, the time, the leaders, the organization, the arrogance to call ourselves 'civilized' and other people 'savage'. What 'primitive' tribe would do this to its own? Put part of them to one side and say 'we don't understand you, you're not like us, you're animals'? What were all these civilized people doing while this place went down the tube? I'm not just talking about our ghostly helpers, people paid to care or not to as the case may be. What about the rest of us? If we had really cared enough would places like this exist?

STEPHEN So then we don't care about each other as much as we should.

OLLY That's an understatement.

STEPHEN And we're not as reluctant to hurt each other as we might be.

OLLY Our track record there is abysmal everywhere you look. We seem to have an infinite capacity for wiping each other out.

STEPHEN Unlike the Indians of Brazil—is that what you're saying?— who are famous for their ability to get along. Or did your friend fall on his own spear?

OLLY No, he was killed by another Indian, from a different tribe. And, yes, their attitude to killing is so matter of fact that it usually shocks civilizados who like to pretend that such things don't go on in our society every day of the week on a scale that would stagger the average savage. To them it's a functional act, without guilt, even if it's someone they're killing from a nearby tribe, someone they are familiar with. They can't see that it's bad. So we call them uncivilized. But I wonder all the same if they would come over here and deliberately incite two groups of people to a pitched battle so that they could make a film of it.

STEPHEN Is that what you did?

OLLY That's what we were there for though most of us didn't know it. It cost a million and a half dollars and the lives of twenty seven Indians from two tribes, one of which was wiped out, which at today's prices isn't bad going. Don't get me wrong. They'd probably have fought it out eventually anyway, they had grudges going back fifty years, and they were being forced into more and more frequent contact because the Brazilians were building a road through the forest, squeezing the Indians out, making them compete for depleted resources. But we, the good guys, engineered it all the same. We even got it to happen before the heavy rains started. Watch out for it. It'll be gripping TV. Two bunches of dagoes slaughtering each other. Where does that leave *us*?

STEPHEN Exactly where we've always been. What do you suggest we do till we learn how to be civilized? When you think we're ready to start putting things right, drop me a line. When you think we're human enough to start tackling the problems, tell them they can start happening again. You're full of shit. And Fitz: what will he *do* when he's survived?
*(Enter FITZ at speed, out of breath, making signs for silence. He remains silent, listening keenly, for a long time. Then he relaxes and flops down.)*

FITZ They nearly had me then. Twenty or thirty of them with torches and that. They shouted out 'Hoy, we're gunna search you.' So I says to myself 'Are you fuck' and off I went. I had fifty yards start on them else I'd never have made it. Is Ali here?

STEPHEN *(Handing him the letter and package.)* I'll collect the things I want.
*(Exit STEPHEN. FITZ opens the letter which is a birthday card. He reads it. He puts the package in his pocket.)*

FITZ She's comin back next week she reckons. Gone to London.

OLLY When was your birthday?

FITZ Tomorrow

OLLY Nineteen?

FITZ Yeh. What's he doing here, Olly?

OLLY I think Ali made him come specially to give you that.
*(Enter STEPHEN.)*

STEPHEN The blankets.
*(He takes them from his sack.)*

OLLY Thanks.

STEPHEN Don't mention it. I'll be running along then.

OLLY Hitching?

STEPHEN Yes.

FITZ Best not go now. You'll get nabbed. They're just lookin for

|  | people like you. Best wait till mornin. |
|---|---|
| STEPHEN | Fuck. |

*(FITZ takes his cane from his pocket, then two oranges, which he holds up.)*

OLLY Genius. Sheer genius.

STEPHEN In that case I'll get some sleep. I'll use Ali's room if nobody objects.

OLLY Of course not. You better take the blankets.

*(STEPHEN takes them and goes.)*

Well? Find us our dreamhouse?

*(FITZ shakes his head and takes out the letter again.)*

It's a sellers' market just now.

FITZ Olly, what's that one? Just that one. Don't look at the rest.

OLLY Which one? Don't get orange all over it.

FITZ There.

OLLY What scrawly handwriting. Tempting. There you are. She can't stop talking about you. Aren't you going to open the present?

*(Fade.)*


# Thirty two

*(The squat. That night. OLLY and FITZ in sleeping bags. In the distance, the sound of firing.)*

OLLY Fitz, you awake?

FITZ Yeh.

OLLY Hear it?

FITZ Yeh.

OLLY How long's it been going on?

FITZ I've just woke up. Is it still dark do you think?

OLLY Dunno. Sounds like another outbreak of peace. Big one.

FITZ I'll see if I can see anything.

*(He gets dressed and goes out. Enter STEPHEN.)*

STEPHEN What's happening?

OLLY Fitz is having a look.

STEPHEN What do you think?

OLLY I think someone's decided to sort out a few intractable problems in Hulme.

*(Enter FITZ.)*

[62]

FITZ  Still dark. But there's a big fire somewhere over that way.

OLLY  What do you think?

FITZ  Start gettin our stuff together in case. I'll go a bit further.

*(Exit FITZ. OLLY and STEPHEN start getting things together.)*

STEPHEN  Where will you go?

OLLY  Dunno.

STEPHEN  Jesus Christ.

OLLY  I'm scared.

*(Sound of breaking glass. They listen intently. It happens again.)*

OLLY  That was near.

*(Enter FITZ, running.)*

FITZ  Let's go. Gang of twenty or thirty workin their way down the street. Get your stuff.

*(STEPHEN dashes upstairs. Frantic haste to collect belongings.)*

FITZ  Get that. Leave that. Let's go.

*(Exit OLLY. Enter STEPHEN.)*

STEPHEN  Rucksack!

*(He grabs it. It spills. He starts to cram things back in.)*

You go.

*(FITZ pulls out his cane and looks at STEPHEN. They look at each other for a second.)*

FITZ  Come on! Leave it!

*(Exeunt. Blackout.)*

# Thirty three

*(The bridge. Sound of demolition work. OLLY, ALI, and FITZ, who is wearing a new fur hat with ear flaps, are watching the demolition.)*

OLLY  Where you going to spend your days now, Ali?

ALI  The people I used to visit. They won't have gone far.

OLLY  What's the matter?

ALI  You two. I can't get over how terrible you look.

FITZ  I want to go back via Levenshulme. There's a bloke I want to see.

ALI  Just make sure you hang on to your hat.

*(They watch.)*

[63]

OLLY  Christ, what a mess!

ALI  Look! TV! Hoi! Up here!

*(They stand making semaphore signs for a minute or two until they lose interest. They watch the demolition a little more.)*

ALI  Let's go. It's bitter up here.

*(They move off.)*

OLLY  Is there a Tesco in Levenshulme?

FITZ  Bound to be.

OLLY  How come you're such a fucking optimist, Fitz?

*(Fade.)*